ᐃᒪᕕᒻᒥ ᐆᒪᔪᑦ ᐱᐊᕋᖕᒋᓪᓗ
IMAVIMMI UUMAJUT PIARANGILLU
ADULT AND BABY ANIMALS IN THE SEA

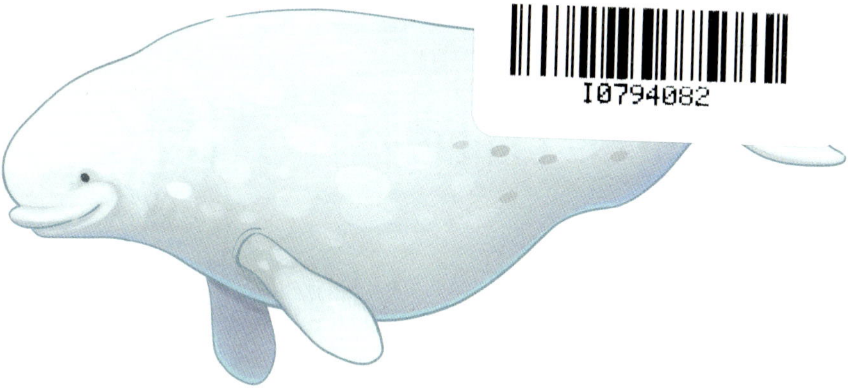

ᑎᑎᖅᑐᒐᖅᑐᖅ

ᐃᒪ ᐲᑐᓴᓐ

TITIQTUGAQTUQ ILLUSTRATED BY

Emma Pedersen

ᐅᓇ ᐊᓪᓚᙳᐊᖅ.

Una allannguaq.

This is a narwhal.

ᐅᓇ ᐅᒋᐊᖅ.

Una ugiaq.

This is a narwhal calf.

ᐅᓇ ᓇᑦᑎᖅ.

Una nattiq.

This is a seal.

ᐅᓇ ᓇᑦᑎᐊᖅ.

Una nattiaq.

This is a seal pup.

ᐅᓇ ᒥᑎᖅ.

Una mitiq.

This is an eider duck.

ᐅᓇ ᒥᑎᕋᖅ.

Una mitiraq.

This is an eider duckling.